Prophetic Fallout of 9-11
The Final Generation

By
Mary Stewart Relfe, Ph.D.
#1 Bestselling Author

*Only one life will soon be past,
Only what's done for Christ will last*

About the Publisher

League of Prayer, Inc. was founded in 1980 by Dr. Mary Stewart Relfe. She serves as President/CEO of *League of Prayer, USA,* an IRS-approved, tax-exempt 501©3 Christian/Humanitarian agency headquartered in Prattville, AL, and *League of Prayer-Russia,* registered in 1992 with headquarters in **Moscow Central Hospital, Moscow, Russia.**

League of Prayer-Russia has operated that nation's largest soup kitchen, the only Christian pre-school; has gone into 400 prisons, many Children's Hospitals, and distributed in excess of a quarter million Bibles.

The ministry has sponsred prison chaplains throughout the state of **Alabama**. It has sponsored ministries in the **Philippines**, supported works in **Scotland**, and assisted in orphanage work in **Moldova and Romania**.

Since 2000, *League of Prayer* has completed 143 homes in **Honduras** for victims of Hurricane Mitch, plus a water system and many flushable latrines. Five schools are being constructed in **Baku, Azerbaijan,** for 4000 refugee children, ages 5-13, who have never attended a class. An **Amputee Care Center** is under construction in **Sierra Leone, W. Africa**, for the fitting of prosthetics on victims of forced amputation by rebel terrorists. It also sponsors a full-time mission in **Madras, India.**

Additionally, *League of Prayer* publishes books, newsletters, and provides Bibles, food, clothes, medicines, vehicles, etc., locally and in other regions beyond.

League of Prayer, Inc.
P.O. Box 680310
Prattville, AL 36068

Phone 334 361 8497
FAX 334 361 9588

E-mail *LofPinc.@aol.com*
www.LeagueofPrayer.org

About the Author

Dr. Mary Stewart Relfe has authored several books. Two were #1 best-sellers, *When Your Money Fails*, (1981), and *The New Money System*, (1982). Both were translated into foreign languages, not a few. She wrote the best-seller *Cure of All Ills—Prayer & Revival*, and has authored other publications including this recent release, *Prophetic Fallout of 9-11*.

Since 1981, Mary has written newsletters that have spanned the globe, some translated into foreign languages. Of late she has edited and published two old manuscripts—*My Sojourn in Heaven & Stopover in Hell*, by John Bunyan, and *Ghosts at the Wesley House*, by Adam Clarke.

Mary has been a lifetime student of the Bible, having read it through dozens of times; lectured on eschatology, hermeneutics, soteriology, and apologetics in educational settings; conducted statewide seminars on prayer, and spoken in many churches in the U.S., Asia and Europe. She has been the pulpit guest in the largest church in the world, Yoido Full Gospel, Seoul, South Korea, at the invitation of Dr. Paul (David) Yonggi Cho in different years.

Mary is a Commercial Pilot and Flight Instructor-multi-engine, instruments, and ground. She has piloted her plane on transcontinental and international flights. She was Montgomery's Woman of Achievement in 1975. By denomination, she is a Wesleyan (Methodist). Her late husband, Dr. C. B. Relfe, M.D., passed away in 1978.

Appreciation

To my mom,

Kathleen Thomas Stewart

You inspired, occupied and dazzled by mind with you literary labors and prowess in prayer. You seemed so small at your rising; yet attained to such a meridian of usefulness and glory, that you appeared broad and resplendent at your setting.

Mom, I never met anyone yet who could name the mothers of David's children, or explain so giftedly the sweet influences of Pleiades and the bands of Orion; or whose prayers were like a cannon set at the entrance of heaven to burst open its gates. Through the immeasurablility of your Bible study and prayer you really did live so near the gate of heaven you eavesdropped — and some of that stardust fell on me.

Solomon must have had you in mind when he wrote: "Many daughters have done virtuously, but thou excelleth them all."

Thanks again mom, who being dead, yet speaketh.

CONTENTS

Chapter I	World Without Money	1
Chapter II	The 666 System Moves On!	9
Chapter III	Decoding the Universal Product Code	23
Chapter IV	WWW.com Languages and 666	35
Chapter V	Last of the "Last Days"	45
Chapter VI	God's Time Clock and our Calendar in Sync?	51
Chapter VI	Mother of All Distresses	63
Capter VII	The Terminal Generation?	67
Chapter VIII	Suggestions for Perilous Times	91

Preface

On September 11, 2001, an apocalyptic event occurred. Readers contacted me and asked: "Where are we in Bible prophecy?" My reply was: "Matthew 24:8: *'All these are the beginning of sorrows.'*"

Count on this: society will never regain a semblance of equilibrium. In light of the bombings and subsequent bio-terrorist attacks, it seemed appropriate to take a step backward and reflect on my studies over the past years.

I wrote two #1 bestselling books in the early 1980s. Methinks they were both 20 years ahead of their time. Some excerpts were republished in 1999. It seems fitting at this juncture to again publish sections from these two books.

The extracts concern the sudden world wide use of the number 666, and its subsequent encoding in the Universal Product Code. According to Bible prophecy, the final economic and religious systems of the last generation will be characterized by this number.

Whatever assessment you make of this presentation is of your own choosing. As for me, I discovered this usage of 666 all around the world. I subsequently decoded the UPC and found 666 in each symbol. To my best judgment, these fulfillments of Bible prophecies are sufficiently convincing to me that — *This generation has a rendezvous with God.*

Chapter I

World Without Money

*"To some generations, much is given.
Of other generations, much is expected.
This generation
has a rendezvous with destiny."*
Franklin D. Roosevelt (1936)

True words, President Roosevelt, amidst the Great Depression, but much more compelling words portray our times. *This generation has a rendezvous with God!*

"This generation shall not pass away, till all be fulfilled"; words spoken by one greater than the president, and believed by hosts of Bible commentators are for our day. (Luke 21:32).

This book purports to present a preponderance of current events since 1948, which fulfill Bible prophecies made thousands of years ago, that identify this generation as *the one which will not pass away until the end comes.*

1

"Tell us when shall these things be? And what shall be the sign of thy coming, and of the end of the world (age)?" the disciples asked Jesus. (Matt. 24:3). His response disclosed many fearful happenings; some which prior generations have experienced. However, there is a uniqueness about this litany of horrors. Many of the events foretold by Jesus (and other prophets), that will signal the end of time as we know it, will all converge on the final generation.

This work is an attempt to focus upon *unprecedented* fulfillments which will only become reality during the last generation of this age.

The Cashless Society

Two prophets in particular, Daniel and the Apostle John, wrote about a unique coalition of nations which would come together and *have one mind*, (Revelation 17:13), during the final 7 years of the terminal generation of this age. All Bible prophecies agree on:—

1. The necessity of this *world government*. In one word: **violence**. *"As it was in the days of Noah, so shall it be also in the days of the (coming of the) Son of man... The earth was corrupt*

2

before God, and the earth was filled with violence," (Luke 17:26 and Gen. 6:11).

In another word: **Inability to govern.** *"And there shall be... upon the earth distress of nations, with perplexity..."* (Luke 21:25). *"Distress of nations"* in the Greek (*synche*) *means "holding fast together in anguish." "Perplexity" (aporia) means "without a passage out." Young's Analytical Concordance with Hebrew & Greek Lexicons.*

One more word: **Fierceness of times.** *"This know also that in the last days perilous times shall come... Evil men and seducers shall wax worse and worse, deceiving and being deceived."* II Tim. 3:1 & 13). *"Perilous" Greek (Chalepas) means fierce, violently hostile, given to fighting or killing, furiously active or determined, unrestrained zeal.*

2. Absolute power the leader (dictator) will wield. *"Power was given him (its leader) over all kindreds, tongues and nations. And all that dwell upon the earth shall worship him, whose names are not written in the book of life... (He will) make war against the saints (believers in God) and overcome them."* Rev. 13:7-8.

He (this last world dictator) is different from all others, exceedingly dreadful. He shall

speak great words against the most High (God), make war with the saints and prevail against them, until the Ancient of days comes.
Dan. 7:19, 21, 25.

This last secular government system will consist of three branches; executive, religious and economic. Its tenure will be seven years, (Daniel's 70th week; a week of years divided in mid-term). Dan. 9:24-27 and Rev. 13:5-17.

The executive branch will be presided over by a ruthless dictator, whom the Jews will accept as their Messiah, though this acceptance is short-lived—3 $1/2$ years. Christians will recognize him as the antichrist, the man of sin, Mr. 666, II Thess. 2:3 and Rev. 13:18. The Minister of the One World Religion will exercise all the power of the dictator, Rev. 13:12. He makes fire come down from heaven and deceives mankind by the miracles he performs, Rev. 13:13-14.

The chief executive and religious leader will themselves oversee a never-tried, innovative, ingenious method of transacting all business. It is a system conducted, not with money, but with marks. Seen as the last resort for prevention of crime, violence and terrorism—it's presumed to be earth's last hope for peace—in an era characterized by *"men's hearts failing them for fear,"* Luke 21:26.

Volumes could be (and have been) written about the political and religious aspects of this government. However, the focus here will be turned on the economy—how finances will be managed during the final seven years of the final generation.

Eliminating cash—imminent

Treasury Secretary Paul O'Neill warns about the dangers of currency as it relates to terrorism.

"Currency can be as lethal as a bullet. If we are to root out terrorist cells that threaten to do violence to our people, we have to hunt the financial benefactors and intermediaries that underwrite murder and mayhem." Paul O'Neill, U. S. Treasury Secretary, on steps being taken to control terrorism.

The message is subtle. To control terrorism, terrorists' money must be controlled.

Hunt them? The U. S. has! And in the process discovered that Osama bin Laden owns banks all over the world. He capitalized his banks with millions of dollars. Most of their current cash flow stems from the opium poppy grown by Afghan farmers. These are paid slave wages to supply 72% of the world's stockpile. From the unripe seed capsules of the opium poppy, codeine, morphine, and a stronger drug than morphine, heroin, are made, and sold for illegal and legitimate purposes. These banks are equipped to electronically transfer funds to any member of his al Qaida network and other associates, who choose to exact terror on the civilized world.

"The only way to eliminate crime is to eliminate cash." F. Lee Bailey, the famed attorney, who has been proclaiming this for years. As have others—two articles follow as evidence.

Almost foolproof cure for crime

"We are witnessing a barrage of news-media concern and debate about violent crime and its effect on the quality of life in the United States. In sheer monetary loss, the cost to society runs into the hundreds of billions of dollars, a substantial fraction of the total federal

budget. Yet there is a simple—or, better, simply stated—solution that would instantly result in a drastic reduction in crime... **The solution is to eliminate cash. We are clearly moving in the direction of a cashless society.** *It has been much discussed—but not... in the context of crime prevention. Think of countless cash-filled shoe boxes and safety-deposit vaults crammed with the results of income-tax fraud, bribery, drug profits and robbery...*

"Consider this: At a predetermined time, all cash would have to be surrendered to banks acting as agents of the Treasury. **Every citizen would be assigned a thief-proof account card... In any case, it is clear that cash is the greatest convenience ever devised to facilitate the commission of crime."** Los Angeles Herald Examiner, *April 28, 1981,* article: <u>Almost Foolproof Cure for Crime: Eliminate Cash</u>, by Leon M. Lederman, Page A 11.

Mr. Lederman's 1981 concept of a *"thief-proof account card"* seems unlikely today with terrorists finding little resistance in acquiring 10 aliases, multiple driver's licenses, and fraudulent passports, etc.

Cashless, paperless... defenseless

This cartoon of the ultimate Cashless System was displayed with the article.

"The cashless society is approaching faster than most people realize... In the quest for the ultimate means of identification, there is talk of branding everyone with a number. Any such action would surely cause an uproar, but as card fraud increases and customers get tired of paying for it in increased costs, it is seen as **the only possible solution**...The vision of the future is the cashless, paperless society where money will move instantaneously and invisibly through a central joint operational centre, and consumers will possess **one card** that will access all financial services. Sydney Morning Herald. (Sydney Australia) February 14, 1984 article titled _Cashless, paperless, defenceless_, by Wayne Dean, p. 9.

Chapter II

The 666 System Moves On!

"And he causeth all, both small and great,
rich and poor, free and bond,
to receive a mark in their right hand,
or in their foreheads;

"And that no man might buy or sell
save he that had the mark, or the name of
the beast, or the number of his name.
Here is wisdom. Let him that hath
understanding count the number of the
beast: for it is the number of a man;
and his number is
Six hundred threescore and six,"

Revelation 13:16-18.

My first book was titled *WHEN YOUR MONEY FAILS — 666.* Published in 1981, it became a best-seller and was translated into foreign languages, not a few. The blatant use of the devil's number, "666," which burst on the world stage in the late 70s, was exposed to readers across the earth. In dozens of pictures I proved how the global economic, political and religious systems were exhibiting the use of the triple digit "666" on their products, credit cards, IRS forms, Vatican admission coupons, etc. A few of the infinite usages are shown in the following pages.

Present use not a jinx

Officials of companies which used this number on products, forms, cards, etc., probably had little to no knowledge of the significance of it, and perhaps would be unable to explain why it appeared in connection with their business. And certainly no evil proceeds from a product or a person who uses it — at this time. Sally O'Brien was not *cursed* because Sears and Penney assigned her a number incorporating "666." Neither did Pepsi suffer any injury for playing the "666" game — nor those who drank Pepsi — which has always been my favorite cola. However, the use of this number should sound an alarm to awaken Christians out of their sleep. It is a solemn warning the world has entered the last of the last days.

They were wrong

Three to four decades ago many preachers were assuring believers that this *man of sin* and his number "666" would not be a factor until after the church was "caught up." Some today still can't accept II Thessalonians 2:3; knowledge has increased, and everything we buy or sell is already in the "666" system.

International corporations joined in the public display of "666" on their products. See top of can. This use was officially explained as *"Pepsi Challenge TV Cash Game 666."*

Changeover at the Pentagon!
The U.S. Defense Dept. Journal,
First Quarter 1983, p.42-43 depicts
a roll-over from an old runner #451,
handing a torch to a new runner
wearing the World Coalition Code
#666. This will be the code for the
global government, the last One
World Government System.

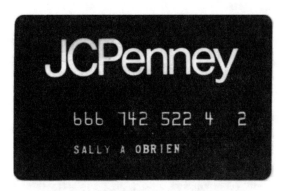

J.C. Penney card issued in 1980 to my
assistant, Sally O'Brien. It's prefixed
with the World Code "666."

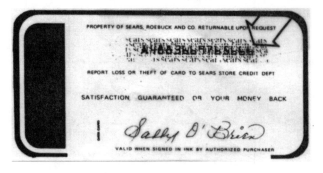

Copy of the back of a Sears card issued
to my assistant, Sally O'Brien in 1978.
It's suffixed with World Code "666." A
multitude of usages of "666" on credit
cards, banking logos, deposit slips, etc.,
are in my files.

Department of the Treasury
Internal Revenue Service

1980

Instructions for
Forms W-2 and W-2P

Box 14.—IRA codes.—If box 9 is an IRA payment, enter 666. Identify the kind of payment by showing one of the following code numbers after 666: 1 for premature (other than disability or death); 2 for rollover; 3 for disability; 4 for death; 6 for other; 7 for normal; 8 for excess contributions plus earnings on such excess contributions; and 9 for transfer to an IRA for a spouse, incident to divorce. (For example, 6663 for disability.)

FOR DISTRICT OFFICE USE

SOCIAL SECURITY OFFICE 666
P.O. Box 178
Lakeland FL 33802

Evidence Reviewed

Interview Conducted Per EM 381.1 ☐

Employee Signature   Title   Date

FOR BUREAU OF DATA PROCESSING

In my file are additional examples of the U.S. government using the number "666." After my book was published, they stopped denying it.

Jerusalem Post, November 25, 1980, pictures an advertisement of a nationwide contest entitled, "Uncover Six Six Six and Win!" Sponsored by the Department of Education and Health Services, it is designed to "educate, prepare, and condition" the Jews to accept these smiling 666s as something not bad, but good! It is the Number of their False Messiah, the Antichrist, and his World Government System. It will be Israel's Final Folly.

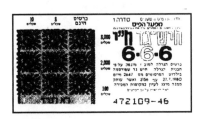

Lottery ticket brought back from Israel in March 1981. A national lottery was being conducted in Israel, and printed on EACH LOTTERY TICKET WERE THE NUMBERS "666."

LSI Computers made in the U.S. and shipped to Israel had on them this seal. After publication of my first book, officials of LSI wrote me that they discontinued the use of "666."

A shirt made in Red China, with the number "666" on the label forming a trademark. This shirt was sold through a jobber in Hong Kong, and purchased through a retail store in Kansas City, MO.

Public transportation tickets sold in Milan, Italy, prefixed "666." The same prefix is on admission tickets to the Vatican!

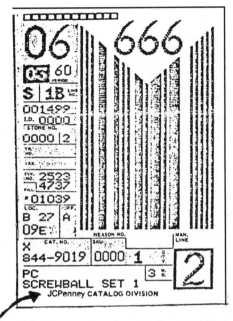

J.C. Penney's screwball set "666."

"666" Product
Identification
System used by
Koehring & Clark
Equipment.

17

**Bottom, Armstrong tile
prefixed front and back "666."**

SIX HUNDRED THREE
SCORE AND SIX

Social Security Number | For Payroll Office Use Only

666

Form 4677 (1-76)

South Central Bell

YOUR SECRET PERSONAL IDENTIFICATION CODE

666 1

This is your code. If you want to change it, mark through all four digits...
...and use the spaces below to write in the four digits you prefer to use.

South Carolina National
Member FDIC

Sears

Sears, Roebuck and Co.
P488366976566

Pacific Northwest Bell

503 485 3045F 666
72 02 131

OFFERS SPECIAL RATES NATIONWIDE
TO CLUB MEMBERS. RECAP NO. 8666666

National Car Rental

DAMIEN 666
OMEN II

There's much more

These are a few of a multitude of examples of the global use of Satan's number "666." Notice its use traverses the political, financial and economic sphere. Why "666?" During this research I sought to determine if there had been historically a wide-spread use of triple digits as 444, 555, etc. It didn't exist. The discovery was weighty. There could be but one deduction. *The wonderful Numberer, Palmoni, The Numberer of Secrets,* had ascertained the hour had arrived for the forces of evil to make antichrist's number "666" fashionable.

References #5516 & #4742 in Strong's Exhaustive Concordance of the words spelled out — six hundred threescore and six = *"chi xi stigma,"* means *"to stick, prick, a mark incised or punched for recognition of ownership — mark."*

Antichrist's PIN

Many times an individual receives a PIN number. In our banking system this is known only to the one to whom it's assigned. The antichrist's PIN # will be known by all — "666." It probably will be in the form of a prefix of a longer number and will be put on the hand or forehead of unbelievers via a *stick, prick or incised mark.*

"666" in a more subtle form

After the publication of this book, there was a public outcry against the entire world (communist and free) utilizing the devil's number. I believe largely in response to the irrefutable proof published in this book, the outward use of "666" quickly went underground.

Psychology Today, **May 1983, with accompanying article projecting the bar code system. With personal bar code on forehead and bar codes on all items, as shown in pictures, scanning products and forehead would facilitate shopping, the article maintains.**

Chapter III

Decoding the Universal Product Code

In my second book, *The New Money System*, (also a #1 best-seller), God enabled me to decode the Universal Product Code Symbols. I discovered each of its UPC designs are framed with the digits "666." The start, center guard, and stop characters are taken from the construction of the digit six. The need for public display of "666" ceased when bar codes (with "666" encoded) were less objectionable.

UPC Design #1 and "666"

The first glimmer in the breaking of the Bar Code Marketing System came when I obtained a Set of Bars representing the numbers 0-9. This Optical Character Recognition (OCR) B font identified "Bars" (Lines or Marks) for Numbers. With this conversion chart of "Bars for Numbers," it became ap-

parent that **two uniform lines** were being
used to depict the number "6" in the Universal Product Code's most commonly used Bar
Code.

FIGURE 1

All bars in the Symbol are identified by numbers at the bottom, except three sets of "two uniform bars" which appear identical to "6."

FIGURE 2

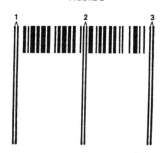

The only bars unidentified by numbers in this basic UPC DESIGN are shown isolated in Positions 1, 2, and 3.

FIGURE 3

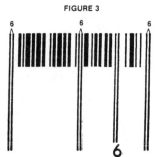

A visual inspection of the three always unidentified bars, compared to the bar UPC identifies as "6" isolated.

These are three sets of bars (representing numbers) used in the UPC designs. For the purpose of explaining "6" in the second exhibit, I shall just say that a single bar in set #3 is used. Anyone interested in 20 pages of intricacies about the construction of the bars in each design can order a copy of *The Money System,* and receive also the response to my letter of inquiry to the Uniform Product Code Council about the reason for using all visible components of digits "6" for the *Left guard, Right guard and Center bar pattern.* (These information bars are 3 and 5-module 6s, while the Data Characters are 7-module 6s).

UPC DESIGN #2 is second most commonly seen UPC DESIGN. All bars identified by numbers beneath Symbol except three.

The single Mark for 6 is from Set 3, which is used here to represent the second 6 in "666."

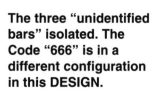

The three "unidentified bars" isolated. The Code "666" is in a different configuration in this DESIGN.

There are other designs in my book, *The New Money System*. For our purposes here, you can go to your kitchen and pick up any can of food, loaf of bread, etc., and easily identify "666" in 95% of your home products, from studying these most popular UPC designs.

Explosion!

After the publication of *The New Money System*, February 1, 1982, cartoonists and journalists around the world took up my cause. A few examples follow.

The Orange County Register, **March 14, 1982.**

"Crowd" identified by bar codes in 1982 Art Contest sponsored by *East New York Savings Bank.*

The Bellingham Herald,
August 8, 1982.

The Tucson Citizen,
April 5, 1982.

Forbes (April 12, 1982): "This month the Pentagon will begin asking its suppliers to use bar codes."

The Boston Herald April 10, 1983.

```
D>67    M77117  666
77117   666    TAUPE  8 D
```

From box of walking shoes "666."

"666" erasers distributed
in elementary schools.

Badges from
U.S. Treasury,
Alcohol,
Tobacco and
Firearms
division, bore
World Code at
bottom "666."

Wall Street Journal, May 23, 1983

The Sydney Morning Herald, Sydney, Australia,
October 1, 1983

In *The Sydney Morning Herald*, February 14, 1984, an article appeared with this same cartoon (shown here) titled *Cashless, paperless, defenseless.* I quote again:

*"The cashless society is approaching faster than most people realize... In the quest for the ultimate means of identification, there is talk of branding everyone with a number. Any such action would surely cause an uproar, but as card fraud increases and customers get tired of paying for it in increased costs, **it is seen as the only possible solution.**"*

William Safire chimes in

The celebrated syndicated columnist wrote an article titled *Here Comes the Computer Tattoo.* He concludes with this solemn warning: *"Though aimed against 'undocumented workers,' **the computer tattoo will be pressed on you and me.**"* (A.P.) August 18, 1983.

Obviously, my first two books awakened a sleeping society and aroused a curiosity in many of this "666" phenomenon.

SIX HUNDRED THREE
SCORE AND SIX

Chapter IV

WWW.com
Languages and "666"

The Internet is a global electronic village called the Information Highway. World Wide Web is the most complete realization of the Internet to date. WWW was developed in the 1990s at the European Center for Nuclear Research, Geneva, Switzerland so that information could be shared. It is a huge collection of sites connected through hyperlinks. You navigate this graphical environment via a web browser. WWW is now in 160 nations. It doubles in size every eight months. Current size: 3 terabytes (3 million megabytes). About 1.5 million Web pages are created every day.

Since this will obviously be the system used by the coming World Dictator, my curiosity sought to discover any linkage to the number "666." The study took me back to the ancient alphabets. In each I learned the letter "W" has a numerical value of 6. Because of the huge size, I am using the top of one of my worksheets.

Gematria

SINAI	MOA-BITE	PHOENICIAN Letters	Classical GREEK	LATIN	
ALEPH (Bull) 1		1 aleph	1 alpha	A	A
BETH (House) 2		2 beth	2 beta	B	B
GIMEL (Square) 3		3 gimel	3 gamma	C	C
DALETH (Door) 4		4 daleth	4 delta	D	D
HALLEL (Rejoice) 5		5 he	5 epsilon	E	E
WAW (Peg) 6		6 vav	6 digamma	F	F

Gematria; the use of letters in the alphabet instead of figures. Arabian numbers 0-9, a comparatively recent creation, were unknown to, and could not have been used by, ancient nations.

36

You will notice the 6th letter, *"ww, yu, vv (double "v" is "w")* and *F* are all assigned the value of 6. Remember there were no vowels. To aid in pronunciation, vowels were added here. The Greeks had such difficulty with the "waw" sound, they left it in the 6th place to mean w with the assigned value of 6, but called it *digamma*.

So the next time you see WWW dot com, think ***"666.com."***

The Hebrew
"Alphanumeric" Alphabet

The Hebrew Alphabet consists of 22 (2x11) letters, so the 5 finals were added to make up three series of 9, or 27 in all:

Aleph	א = 1	Yod	י = 10	Koph	ק = 100	
Beth	ב = 2	Kaph	כ = 20	Resh	ר = 200	
Gimel	ג = 3	Lamed	ל = 30	Shin	ש = 300	
Daleth	ד = 4	Mem	מ = 40	Tau	ת = 400	
He	ה = 5	Nun	נ = 50	Koph	ך = 500	
Vau	ו = 6	Samech	ס = 60	Mem	ם = 600	Finals.
Zayin	ז = 7	Ayin	ע = 70	Nun	ן = 700	
Cheth	ח = 8	Pe	פ = 80	Pe	ף = 800	
Teth	ט = 9	Tsaddi	צ = 90	Tsaddi	ץ = 900	

The Greek
"Alphanumeric" Alphabet

The Greek letters were 24, and the required number, 27, was made up by using the final "s" or s (called *Stigma*) for 6, and adding two arbitrary symbols called respectively *Koppa*, for 90, and *Sampsi*, for 900.

Alpha	α = 1	Iota	ι = 10	Rho	ρ = 100
Beta	β = 2	Kappa	κ = 20	Sigma	σ = 200
Gamma	γ = 3	Lambda	λ = 30	Tau	τ = 300
Delta	δ = 4	Mu	μ = 40	Upsilon	υ = 400
Epsilon	ε = 5	Nu	ν = 50	Phi	φ = 500
Stigma	ς = 6	Xi	ξ = 60	Chi	χ = 600
Zeta	ζ = 7	Omicron	ο = 70	Psi	ψ = 700
Eta	η = 8	Pi	π = 80	Omega	ω = 800
Theta	θ = 9	*Koppa*	Ϟ = 90	*Sampsi*	ϡ = 900

Rome did it their way

The Romans didn't use all the letters of their alphabet for numerals, as did the Greeks and Hebrews. They used only six! It is both remarkable and significant that these total 666.

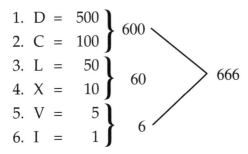

Think of how difficult it would be to multiply, subtract or divide in Roman Numerals. These are still in common use for special emphasis. Big business could not have been conducted until after 773 A.D. when the Arabian Numbers were introduced to the West.

Root values of alphabets

That "spirit of Palmoni, the numberer of secrets," inspires me as I give myself to researching the numerical significance found lying hidden in the languages. There were forerunners of antichrist, for example, *Antiochus IV*, who sacrificed a pig on the altar in Jerusalem, forbade circumcision, destroyed all Old Testaments he could find, placed an idol in the Holy of Holies, and took for himself the title "*God Manifest*." In Greek, this is called *Epiphaneia*. Its numerical value is "666." Many such examples are given in my book, *When Your Money Fails, 666*.

English, too

English, like the oldest alphabet discovered, is based on a root value of 6. For example, 6x2 = 1 foot; 6x6 = 1 yard; 6 forties = 1 section; 6x6 sections = 1 township; 1 township is a 6-mile square.

Man's number

Man's number in the Scripture is "6." The square of 6 = 36. The sum total of all numbers in this square, 1+2+3+5… +35+36 = 666. Unfortunately, Satan's number in the Bible is also 6.

God created man on the 6th day. He completed His work on the 6th day. Man has obviously been given six (thousand-year) days to complete his. We are in the age of "6."

The English alphabet was not designed *purposely* to be alphanumeric. However, when 6 is assigned to the first letter A, and six is added to each succeeding letter, some very intriguing combinations have been uncovered.

ENGLISH ALPHABET & GEMATRIA

A = 6	I = 54	R = 108
B = 12	J = 60	S = 114
C = 18	K = 66	T = 120
D = 24	L = 72	U = 126
E = 30	M = 78	V = 132
F = 36	N = 84	W = 138
G = 42	O = 90	X = 144
H = 48	P = 96	Y = 150
	Q = 102	Z = 156

C = 18	M = 78
O = 90	A = 6
M = 78	R = 108
P = 96	K = 66
U = 126	**258**
T = 120	
E = 30	O = 90
R = 108	F = 36
666	**126**

	B = 12
	E = 30
	A = 6
	S = 114
	T = 120
	282
	666

S = 114
O = 90
N = 84

O = 90
F = 36

S = 114
I = 54
N = 84
___
666

A = 6

S = 114
K = 66
Y = 150

J = 60
A = 6
C = 18
K = 66
I = 54
N = 84
G = 42
___
666

A = 6
T = 120
T = 120
A = 6
C = 18
K = 66

B = 12
Y = 150

A = 6
I = 54
R = 108
___
666

N = 84
E = 30
W = 138

Y = 150
O = 90
R = 108
K = 66
___
666

Chapter V

Last of the "Last Days"

"Knowing this first, that there shall come in the last days scoffers, walking after their own lusts,

"And saying, 'Where is the promise of his coming?' for since the fathers fell asleep, all things continue as they were from the beginning of the creation,"

II Peter 3:3-4.

How many times has it been said, "Oh I've heard that since time immemorial." It signifies two things: First, when one alleges this, it is another sign that these are the last days! Second, it isn't true.

We need only to focus upon this generation and name events unique to it, which have never occurred before, and without which Bible prophecies would not be fulfilled, Christ could not return, and the Age could not be consummated presently.

Sequence of the terminal generation

1. *1948, Israel* regained possession of their home land. Christ could not have come again until this event transpired.

2. *Computers concurrently* began to increase in number. Without this invention, there could be no global infrastructure, no One-World Government, which must be implemented the last 7 years (Daniel's 70th week); the first $3 \frac{1}{2}$ years the antichrist persecutes believers; the last $3 \frac{1}{2}$ years the world experiences the wrath of God. Dan. 7:21, 25-27; 9:27 and Rev. 13:7-8.

3. *March 1973*, the Uniform Product Code Council met, organized, and articulated an agenda which would accommodate a worldwide high-technology economic system destined to be cashless; central to which would be a bar code, whose symbols would be framed by the digits "666."

4. *Fall 1973*, education of cashless future began with young people. *Senior Scholastic*, a magazine for high school students, shows a full-color artist's rendering of youths from various parts of the world with their numbers tattooed on their foreheads. Excerpts of an article in this issue, *"Public Needs and Private Rights — Who is Watching You?"* are quoted here:

"All buying and selling in the program will be done by computer. No currency, no change, no checks. In the program people would receive a number that had been assigned them tattooed in their wrist or forehead. The number is put on by a laser beam and cannot be felt. The number in the body is not seen with the naked eye and is as permanent as fingerprints. All items of consumer goods will be marked with a computer mark. The computer outlet in the store which picks up the number on the items at the checkstand will also pick up the number in the person's body and automatically total the price and deduct the amount from the person's 'Special Drawing Rights' account..." (See picture.)

COVER COPY of SENIOR SCHOLASTIC,
September 20, 1973, an excellent secular
high school publication depicting the future
"buying and selling" system, with numbers
inserted on the foreheads of the youth of
the world.

It was necessary for this remarkable economic innovation to be conceived and executed before this Age ends. In its refined form, all buying and selling will be conducted the last 7 years of the terminal generation in the absence of money — just "marks" — on the right hand or forehead. Rev. 13:16-18

5. *1977 onward*, the knowledge of the UPC symbol with its 3 sets of uniform bars representing three "6s" burst upon the world stage. Political, economic and religious kingpins, desiring to bring to fruition this global era of prosperity, excitedly began placing the number on about everything. *It was in vogue to use "666."* Canada's Prime Minister Pierre Trudeau, known for his efforts of promoting the One-World Government, wore "666" on the license plate of his personal car. (Picture in book, *The New Money System.*)

6. *1980s on* — saw perilous times, threat of global nuclear war, biological warfare, violence filling the earth, men's heart failing them for fear. Such terror, and

threats of terror, had never existed before this generation in such magnitude.
Jesus declared there had never been a
time like it before, or ever would be
again, Mat. 24:21. Paul indicated that in
the last days horrors would accelerate,
and *"Evil men and seducers shall wax
worse and worse."* II Tim. 3-13.

7. *1990, World Wide Web*, the method by
    which th World Dictator can keep
    records on every individual on earth and
    monitor every one's financial transac-
    tions. Its address? **666dotcom.**

    I believe the terminus of the terminal
    generation is upon us living today. Only
    two significant prophetic events have
    yet to occur for the last 7 years of this
    Age to commence.
    * The revealing of the antichrist,
      II Thes. 2:3, and,

    * The covenant he must negotiate with
      Israel for 7 years, Dan. 9:27. (Concur-
      rent with this will be a rebuilt Jewish
      Temple).

Chapter VI

God's Time Clock & Our Calendar in Sync?

What year is it on God's timepiece? How well does our Gregorian calendar, which dates from the birth of Christ, accommodate the Lord's 360 day years?

Since time immemorial folk have by hook or crook kept abreast of time. South American tribes expected Spring when the Pleiades rose. North American Indians knew it was time to plant corn when oak buds reached the size of a squirrel's ear.

The Sumerians of Babylonia were the first to create a calendar. They used 12 months and added an extra month every 4 years. Problems arose when summer months came in spring.

Realizing the calendar needed a major overhaul, Julius Caesar, with the assistance of an astronomer (Sosigenes), adjusted the calendar. His calendar consisted of 365-day years with an extra day every four years — Leap Year. A month was named in honor of Emperor Julius' work — July.

Caesar Augustus seized upon the moment and furthered the refining process. Not to be outdone by Julius, he changed the month following July to 31 days also and named it for himself — August.

By 1545, the vernal equinox was 10 days out of phase. Soon afterwards, Pope Gregory XIII corrected the error, and the calendar used today was named in his honor. It was adopted by Roman Catholic countries in 1582. Not until 1752 would England (which had its own Anglican religion) begin to use it. By this time it was necessary to drop 11 days. October 4 became October 15. Masses of English folk so resented it, they walked in processions crying: *"Give us back our 11 days."* Eastern Orthodox would not accept it until 1923. They had to drop 13 days. China adopted it in 1929.

The Jews began reckoning time in 3761 B.C., the Greeks in 776 B.C., the Romans in 753 B.C., the Muslims in 622 A.D. Christians date time from the birth of Christ, but *the practice wasn't begun until the 6th century A.D.*

Herein lies the jinx. At the time Christians demanded the calculation of time begin at the birth of Jesus, the accuracy of the Julian calendar was in dispute. Christians and secular historians, scientist and astronomers place the birth of Christ from 7-4 B.C. If the Gregorian calendar, which the world of Christians and commerce use, is off by 4 -7 years, then it's of no significant consequence. And, especially when an effort is made to conform our 365 1/4 days a year with God's lunar reckoning throughout Scripture, and the prophetic years of 360 days.

Prophetic implications here are rife. Follow me carefully. Daniel proclaimed to King Nebuchadnezzar: *"He (God) changes the times and seasons,"* Daniel 2:21. When the spring equinox arrives, it is God who rolls earth's axis, and the time and season change from winter. The Lord decreed in Genesis 8:22: *"While the earth remains, seedtime and harvest, cold and heat, summer and winter, and day and night shall not cease."* Times and seasons are in God's power.

Dire implications for Christian calendar

Daniel speaks prophetically about the coming *World Dictator*, antichrist, Mr. 666: "*He shall speak great words against the most High, and shall wear out the saints of the most High, and **think to change times and laws...**"* Daniel 7:25. A more liberal rendering is — he will change times and religious laws for 3 1/2 years.

Terrorism will play a prominent role in the rise of the antichrist. Mass confusion, up-heaval, frustration, economic chaos, civil unrest, violence and monetary instability will pave the road for the rise of the madman of the ages, antichrist. He will march on the stage speaking swelling words: *"I have the answers to these questions. I have the solutions to these problems. I have the remedy for these evils. I have the cure of these ills. Trust me!"*

In his platform will be a petition to the World Court which will solve this calendar problem once and for all and for everybody. It will no longer be offensive to non-Christians. Today, commerce around the world is conducted using the (Christian) Gregorian calendar. Muslim businessmen can't purchase stock without keying in their computers, say January 1, 2002 A.D. (anno domini). Anno = year; domini = Lord, master. Any significant business transaction — document, invoice, etc. — has emblazoned on it: in the year of our Lord.

Antichrist will seek to become politically correct by ridding the calendar of any reference to the Christian faith, in his supposed sympathy for Muslims, atheists, Hindus, Buddhists, etc.

"So we have seen and proved that what the prophets said came true. You will do well to pay close attention to everything they have written for, like lights shining into dark corners, their words help us to understand many things that otherwise would be dark and difficult," **II Peter 1:19. TLB.**

The Numberer of Secrets

I'd like to better introduce you to *Palmoni*. He is a Watcher, a holy Angel, who is in charge of the arithmetic of God. He presides over the numerics in the Scriptures — the things which have to do with numbers regarding time — numbers of minutes, hours, days and years. One commentator suggested Palmoni is in charge of a staff of angels whose duties are to make certain events take place precisely within the divinely scheduled number of days, years, etc.

Daniel 8:13 identifies Palmoni as "that certain saint." In the margins of Reference Bibles is given his title out of the Hebrew: *The Numberer of Secrets,* or, *The Wonderful Numberer.* It then relates his name: *Palmoni.*

"That certain saint" refers one to —

Daniel 4:13 where he is called *"a watcher and a holy one."*

Daniel 4:17 in which he is grouped with *"watchers."*

Daniel 4:23 called a *"a watcher and a holy one."*

Daniel 12:6 "clothed in linen upon the waters."

The questions posed in 8:13 and 12:6 involve *numbers of days* until an event occurs: the first answer being 2,300 days, the second 3 1/2 years.

"Pala" in Hebrew (Strong's Exhaustive

Concordance #6381) means *"great, wonderful, hard, hidden, things too high, (to show marvelous things, work), miracles."* #6382 — *"wonderful"*; #6383 — *"secret, wonderful."*

How thrilling to study about *The Numberer of Secrets, The Wonderful Numberer!* God watches over His word to perform it, and to make sure He is always on time. To do so, He has provided Himself with capable assistants, *wonderful numberers*!

Dare I admit that at times I have felt a kinship with Palmoni? These past 20 plus years have found me endeavoring to discover the *wonderful secrets* of numbers recorded in Scripture.

"Watch" the marketplace

Jesus used this word *watch* often. *"Watch and pray,"* (Luke 21:36); *"Watch you therefore,"* Mark 13:35. In referencing Palmoni's *watchers,"* the crossover into Greek leads one to some intriguing conclusions. Everyone is familiar with prayer — the only power on earth that commands the power of heaven. But who has plumbed the tenor of that other word Jesus used before prayer — *watch*? It has a profound message for the end-times.

Watch World Trade Center?

Strong's Exhaustive Concordance traces the watchfulness down to #58: *"Watch the town square... watch the marketplace."* In looking up marketplace, we find it *"was used for a variety of purposes other than the sale of products. It was a place where business deals were made."* More business trades were made in the Twin Towers than any place on earth!

Methinks when Jesus said *"watch and pray,"* He meant for us to *watch merchandising, watch commerce, watch business, watch buying and selling, and yes, today, for us to watch terrorists.* When we watch these things, we shall know better how to pray as we ought in these times ahead.

"It is the glory of God to conceal a thing, but the honor of kings is to search out a matter," Proverbs 25:2. In searching out the secrets of the Word, we are not only doing a royal but an honorable work.

Wave of the future

Virtual banks are already making their presence felt and are changing the financial landscape. These, as *Security First Network Bank* in Atlanta, will pioneer the transition from real money to the inevitable cashless era. It's called **Internet banking**, enabling users to download store-bought software on their computers and look at account balances and cleared checks, view and reconcile account balances, transfer funds and pay bills while online. These will have everything but the real thing—cash.

In October 1998, the late Dr. Willard Cantelon spoke with me and correlated the fragility of the world's currencies with the amazing advancement of the implantable microchip. Willard faxed me information about some of the rich and famous now wearing the chip just underneath the skin. One microchip the size of a grain of rice can contain a person's history — financial, medical, and social, and denote his exact whereabouts, while monitoring his every financial transaction. This chip can contain information equal to *30 complete sets of the Encyclopedia Britannica!* Hmm. How this relates to the former Treasury Secretary, Robert Rubin's design of *"a new financial architecture for international finance"* will become unclouded as we continue.

Never lose sight of this fact: In the final world system of commerce — all buying and selling — will not be conducted with money, but with *"marks."* In this high-tech global financial structure, there will be no need for money for the masses. The few who arranged this experiment will have confiscated the real thing, and substituted for it a mark of identification. Revelation 13:16 KJV. How thoughtful of them!

On toward "666"

In *Tragedy and Hope,* **Dr. Carrol Quigley admits:** *"There does exist... an international network whose aim it is to create a world system of financial control in private hands, able to dominate the political system of each country and the economy of the world. The individual's freedom and choice will be controlled within the very narrow alternatives, by the fact that he will be numbered from birth and followed as a number until his death."*

This *new financial architecture*, this new *method without money*, will swiftly evolve into the *"Mark of the Beast."* The apostle John prophesied about this unique method of regulating business transactions before the sages of the world ever envisioned a system of numbers from 0-9. Until the 8th century after Christ, letters of the alphabet (Gematria) were used to denote numerical values! And who could have ever fathomed a computing device in biblical times? Imagine adding, multiplying and dividing in Roman numerals. We've come a long way, believers.

Those espousing the One-World Government have long coveted a major global disruption as justification for confiscating all money and real wealth, and replacing it with *electronic dollars, virtual money.* The upheaval precipitated by terror will usher in that new fiscal system, central to which will be *improved computers* which can calculate trillions of these Arabian numbers 0-9 in a second. *"Here is wisdom. Let him that hath understanding count the number... six hundred, threescore and six,"* Revelation 13:18. The end result *is total people control.*

Chapter VII

Mother of all Distresses

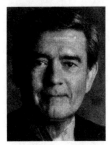

Dan Rather, CBS anchorman, says: "Terrorism and these anthrax attacks are just the beginning."

*"It will be a time of great distress; there has never been such a time from the beginning of the world until now, and will never be again. If that **time of troubles** were not cut short, no living thing could survive; but for the sake of God's chosen, it will be cut short."* Matthew 24:21-22 NEB.

"It certainly seems to me that we're in for something we're not ready for as a nation." Senator Fred Thompson, (R-TN) *Terrorism war spawns silence,* USA TODAY, September 23, 1998.

"The public needs to be aware of the fact that we're moving into an era when casualties from terrorism will become part of daily life, just like car accidents or street crime. " Rapheal Peri, senior analyst on terrorism at

Congressional Research Service.

Anthrax for sale — cheap

By now the terrorist activities of folk like Osama bin Laden are known by all. His car/truck bombs have escalated into suicide bombers hijacking planes loaded with innocent passengers killing thousands. However, *these are just the beginning of sorrows!*

What I'm about to share is more despicable. According to the *Sunday Times* (London), *"Lethal biological germs — anthrax, e-coli, botulinum, brucelia and salmonella — are being sold on the open markets — no questions asked. These weapons of mass destruction have the potential to wipe out cities, states, and entire national populations, if placed in the air, water, or food supply.*

"Labs manufacturing these germs are in eastern Europe and the Third World. A laboratory in Indonesia exports these to North Korea, where the military is known to have- developed huge arsenals of anthrax and botulinum toxins."

Anyone can buy or order by mail

"Laboratories make no checks on custom-

ers. One can even purchase the germs by mail order! Undercover agents for The Sunday Times were offered samples for as little as $20. No questions were asked about flow how the toxins would be used." The Times reported: **"Microscopic quantities can kill hundreds if inhaled or eaten in food.** Cults, terrorists, or psychopaths could spray the germs at crowds or poison water or air-conditioning systems.

"These germs (microorganisms) are the least expensive way to terminate entire populations! This weapon is highly prized in the hands of terrorists, and could well be more lethal than nuclear bombs. The weapon is silent. It can't be detected by X-ray machines at airports. It gives no warning. It's not preceded by a blast. But it could leave hospitals swamped and millions in great cities with hideously blistered faces dying in the streets."

An official at the UN said: "It's easier to get stuff like this than it is to get prescription drugs over the counter."

According, to *PBS Frontline*, Russia has stockpiled these for years. Journalist Richard Grenier posed an unsettling idea. "These could be prepared to kill millions by being disseminated in the air by cans of hair spray."

The Four Horsemen
of the
Apocalypse

"I believe the four horsemen of the apocalypse are already out of the barn. They're saddled up; they're riding. The last horsemen is about death and the animals... I saw that the word **death** means **pestilence** or **disease**. And I thought, 'Where does E. coli come from? Animals!'

"I believe we have been teaching people an escapism gospel. I believe the Bible teaches clearly that the church will go through the tribulation. Pretribulation rapture is a fairly new theology... As I studied the Bible from Genesis to Revelation, I couldn't find one man or woman of God who lived **a charmed life**. All I could find were **fiery furnaces, lion's dens, deserts and pits**." Jim Bakker, *The Re-education of Jim Bakker*, Christianity Today, December 7, 1998.

Chapter VII

The Terminal Generation?

*"I heard behind me a great voice
as a trumpet, saying... write."*
Revelation 1:10-11

Your kindness will surely indulge me for a moment. Many years of my life it's been my privilege to be *"holed up"* with both the written and the Living Word. *"Nobody ever outgrows Scripture. The Book widens and deepens with our years,"* said Charles Spurgeon.

The Bible is awesome! I have treaded on the heels of Daniel, who faints at the voice of the Holy Ones; I have followed the thundering Naham, when his horses plough the waters; sympathized with Habbakuk, when he sees the tents of Cushan in affliction; contemplated with Malachi, the earth burning like an oven; received solace from the pages of

John, who tells of love; climbed the rugged chapters of Peter, who declares the heavens and the earth will be burned up; deliberated on Jude, who launches anathemas upon unbelievers; and stalked John, the Revelator, who heard and wrote facts stranger than fiction.

Now can I say thanks for that divine prompting which set in motion within me a fervor to inherit the unexplored in God? Whoever has claimed all His promises, scaled all His heights and seen His last star? My purpose has been to possess the depths of His riches, to walk where most haven't, and climb where most won't.

In giving myself to vigorous study and research, I too have discerned the voice of *"the king eternal, immortal, invisible, the only wise God."* Does not that same voice which spoke to John come to us and say, "Write?" What is our pen doing? If it's bringing enlightenment to the hearts of others, then angels may tune their hearts when we sit at our desk. They may gladly look upon our pen as writing music for them to sing.

So, buckle up. Fasten your seat belts. Let's explore some of the wonders in the linkage of current events and Bible prophecy, and the fulfillment of end-time Scriptures. And, as we proceed, may God impart wisdom and gird us with strength as those in ancient days, who thought it not robbery to speak God's word and ply his trade; who fainted not at lions' dens, kings' dungeons, swords, or scaffolds. May we discover how to access His pavilion until the storm passes over. For the *fearful and unbelieving* are an affront to God. *The Lord our God in the midst of us — even in these perilous times — is mighty!*

The "genea"

"This generation (genea) should not pass, till all these things be fulfilled," Matthew 24:34.

What generation? The one which would see the budding again of the fig tree. *"Now learn a parable of the fig tree: When his branch is tender and putteth forth leaves, you know that summer is nigh. So likewise, when you shall see ALL these things, know that it (He) is near, even at the doors,"* Matthew 24:32-33.

Learn a parable! A parable illustrates a truth where one thing is said, but another is meant. Why? *"Because it is given unto you to* *know the mysteries* of the kingdom of heaven, but to them it is not given, "* Matthew 13:11. *"Unto you it is given to **know the mysteries** of the kingdom of God, but to others in parables,"* Luke 8:10. Believers are *"stewards of the mysteries of God,"* I Corinthians 4:1.

In Matthew 24, Mark 13 and Luke 21, the parable of the fig tree is recorded, and Jesus likened it to his coming again and the close of this Age. Trees in scriptures are symbolic of great men, peoples and nations. Nebuchadnezzar dreamed of a tree which reached to heaven, (Daniel 4:11). Daniel interpreted the dream: *"The tree which thou sawest... it is thou, O king,"* (Daniel 4:22).

Christ cursed the fig tree, emblematic of cutting off Israel for their refusal to bear fruit. A volume could be written about Old and New Testament scriptures equating Israel with the fig tree. Not only is the fig tree representative of Israel, figs represent Jews!

In Jeremiah, chapter 24, the Lord describes the good and bad figs as good and evil Jews. In 24:5, *the good figs are the good Jews carried away to Babylon whom God would preserve.* In 24:8-9, *the evil figs (Jews) are dispersed over the world, reproached, taunted and cursed.*

70

The people living at the time of Israel's rebirth will see all this litany of evils Jesus listed in verses preceding Matthew 24:32, Mark 13:28 and Luke 21:31. Jesus declared that *"the generation which sees the beginning of these signs (Israel blossoming again as a nation) will see the end of them."*

What a day!

May 14, 1948, Mother gathered us children around her, not an unusual activity for her. It was a customarily repeated act every morning and evening where days began and ended with Bible study and prayer. But this was a special session. Mother, a Bible scholar by anyone's standards, said: *"The most important event since the birth of Christ occurred today! The Jews have a nation again after 2500 years! It was named Israel, not Zion, by only one vote majority in the United Nations."* She continued: *"This is the beginning of the last generation Jesus spoke much about. The consummation of all things is upon us. Jesus could not return, the Church Age could not end, until the Jews were back in their homeland.*

"Now little children look up, lift your face like a flint toward heaven and seize the moment.

It will be the church's finest hour. During these perilous times, Jesus will stand by your side when you know it not. He will encircle every event of your lives with His everlasting arms. He will remove from your path many hurtful things. He will gild every cloud with a merciful lining. So, we'll face these years with songs of praise, power, majesty and might —

> *"Organs, hymns, drums, guitars, and anthems swell,*
>
> *For His church is triumphant, alive and well!"*

I was a mere youth, but as that old song declares: *"I Never Shall Forget That Day!"*

How long is a generation?

The terminal generation began in 1948, and those who saw the beginning of these *special signs* will live to see the end of them. The $64,000 question is — how long will this generation be?

Many sincere believers have made erroneous calculations. Some have judged a generation to be 40 years. Such concluded Jesus had to return by or before 1988.

What the Bible says

There are many *root* words translated *generation* in the Bible. The first reference to generation with respect to time is Genesis 15:16. *"In the fourth generation they (Abraham's descendants) shall come hither again."* God spoke this to Abram in a dream regarding the time his seed would be afflicted in Egypt — *"400 years,"* verse 13. Here a generation (*"dor-cycle"*) was 100 years.

But, in Exodus 12:40 we read: *"The sojourning of the children of Israel, who dwelt in Egypt, was four hundred and thirty years,"* Without a hermaneutical interpretation here, which isn't warranted for our purpose, we can be assured the first generation defined in the Bible ranged from 100 to 107.5 years.

All scriptural usages of generation did not have to do with an assignment of years, as *"O generation of vipers,"* Matthew 3:7.

What the New Testament teaches

"So, all the generations from Abraham to David are fourteen generations; and from

David until the carrying away into Babylon are fourteen generations; and from the carrying away into Babylon unto Christ are fourteen generations," Matthew 1:17.

This word *generation* is from the Greek *"genea."* On the surface that verse does not appear complex. But, *we must study to show ourselves approved **unto God**, a worker, not ashamed, rightly dividing the word of truth,"* II Timothy 2:15.

From many hours of research, I have prepared a chart on *generations* in the New Testament that assigns years to a *genea* in the Old Testament. The dates used are from Archbishop Ussher of Armagh in A.D. 1650-1654, and first put in Bible margins in 1701; and Prof. Willis J. Beecher in his *Dated Events of the Old Testament History*, the most scholarly study of the subjects including the Assyrian Canon. Where secular history is recorded of events included in the Scriptures, these dates coincided.

With respect to both scholars, Ussher and Beecher, where their dates differ a few years, an average between the two were used, as Ussher places Abram's birth at

1996 B.C., Beecher puts it at 2003 B.C. *I used 2000 B.C.* Where David's birth was placed at 1095 B.C. by Ussher, Beecher puts it at 1102. *I used 1100 B.C. See next page.*

GENERATION — Greek = genea
How long is a generation?

Matthew 1:17 —

Generations (*genea*) from Abraham to David are 14; from David to the carrying away into Babylon are 14; from the carrying away into Babylon to Christ are 14.

Abram born in	2000 B.C.
David born in	1100 B.C.
	$900 \div 14 = 64$
Length of generation	**= 64 years**
David born in	1100 B.C.
Babylonian captivity	597
	$503 \div 14 = 36$
Length of generation	**= 36 years**
Babylonian captivity	597
To Christ	00
	$597 \div 14 = 43$

Length of generation = 43 years

Matthew 24:34 —

"This *generation (genea)* shall not pass till all these things be fulfilled." Same word used in Matthew 1:17.

Parable of fig tree (Israel)	1948
Longest generation in N.T.	64
Most far-out date	2012

I'm not declaring the coming of Christ and the subsequent end of this Age by or before 2012, but I have strong leanings toward this. All the signs have converged upon this generation. Jesus said: *"When you shall see these things come to pass, know that it (He) is nigh, even at the doors... (for) this generation shall not pass, till **all** these things be done,"* Mark 13:29-30.

If any is contentious about this, we could go back to Genesis and say the generation could continue for 100 years after 1948. But, that Hebrew term was *"dor,"* not *"genea."* The longest generation in the New Testament is about 64 years!

Believers will know the times

Jesus said, *"As it was in the days of Noah, so shall it be **also** in the days of the (coming of the) Son of Man,"* Luke 17:26. There is a myriad of applications with respect to this reference. Not the least is one where God discloses to Noah the week **the flood would begin**. *"For yet seven days and I will cause it to rain upon the earth forty days and forty nights,"* Genesis 7:4.

If Jesus meant what He said, some of us could know the *very week* of His return. For years I have believed what D.L. Moody said: *"One can live so near the gate of heaven he can eavesdrop."*

Not coming as thief to church

Paul was indignant about the ignorance of Thessalonian believers concerning the Lord's return. He scolded them — *"You brethren are not in darkness that that day should overtake you as a thief,"* as it will unbelievers. His disgust rose to such proportions that he began the chapter — *"But of the times and seasons... you have **no need that I write unto you.**"* I Thessalonians 5:1-4.

If Christ isn't coming to the believer as a thief, then we shall know not only the generation but the approximate time. *No, not the hour or the day!* Christians have used this to justify their silence on this most important topic. It is so imperative to teach about the Lord's return.

◆ *"Unto them that **look** for Him shall He appear the second time..."*
Hebrews 9:28.

◆ *"**Looking** for that blessed hope, and the glorious appearing of the great God and our Saviour Jesus Christ,"* Titus 2:13.

◆ *"**Looking** for and hasting unto the coming of the day of God,"* II Peter 3:12.

◆ *"**Watch** therefore, for you know not what hour your lord doth come... for in such an hour as you think not the Son of Man cometh."* Mat. 24:42 & 44.

◆ *"And what I say unto you, I say unto all, **Watch**,"* Mark 13:37.

◆ *"If therefore thou shalt not watch, I will come on thee as a thief, and thou shalt not know what **hour** I will come upon thee,"* Rev. 3:3.

Where are those with courage and skill on whom God can depend to instruct believers the consequences of not looking and watching? When the Lord *strangely warmed* my heart to write another book, my stout discernment was to *cry aloud, spare not, lift up my voice like a trumpet.* And, *we ought to obey God rather than men.*

This great void in teaching about current events that are dovetailing into fulfillments of Bible prophecy is the reason Jesus could say, *"They ate, drank, married, bought, sold, planted and built to the very day the flood came - and Sodom was destroyed. Even thus it shall be in the day* **when the Son of Man is revealed"** Luke 17:26-30.

Imagine people being so out of sync with the times that there will be marriages consummated the morning Jesus returns. There will be crops being planted with folks expecting a harvest. Houses will be under construction and families will be in anticipation of occupying them. Never a thought of Peter's warning, *"The end of all things is at hand, be ye therefore sober and watch unto prayer,"* I Peter 4:7.

Not coming in famine

Also, Jesus is not returning in a time of famine, (though famine will have preceded the Advent). There will be plenty to eat, drink, buy, sell, plant and build. The madman, antichrist, will pick up the pieces left from the terrorism upheaval, debt, economic collapse, and *"he shall prosper... and shall destroy the mighty and the holy people, and through his policy also he shall make craft to prosper..."* Daniel 8:24-25.

Did others know?

I did this teaching using the chart on an Atlanta television station recently. A sister of my friend, Philip Cameron — Louise, called me a week later. She told me she had just viewed TLC's production titled *Lost Civilization*.

She related that, *"In the 3-hour special, many predictions carved in stone were examined by archeologist and scientists of some renown. Each projection using lunar (moon) cycles which had been deciphered had proved to be accurate — even up to our time — though the civilization became extinct many centuries back. She said the last prediction made was interpreted —* **End of world** *— December 23, 2012.*

Great historian looks at endtime

The History of the Rise & Fall of the Roman Empire, (chapter 15) by Edward Gibbon (1737-1794), has much enamored me. It is an overview of the impact primitive Christianity, *with its austere morals and miraculous powers,* had on the Roman Empire. Since not many will have access to this book or pull it off the Internet, my conscience would shame me for not sharing a few choice observations before the main course.

III The Church was powerful with its supernatural gifts — *"Tongues, visions, prophecy, the power of expelling daemons, healing the sick, raising the dead and the knowledge of foreign languages... These were very liberally bestowed on all ranks of the faithful, on women as on elders, on boys as well as upon bishops... Visions were, for the most part, to disclose the future or to guide the present administration of the church. The expulsion of daemons from the bodies of those whom they had been permitted to torment... was considered the* **most convincing evidence of the truth of Christianity.**

"The 2nd century was still more fertile in miracles than the first... From the first of the fathers to the last of the popes, a succession of bishops, saints, martyrs and of miracles is continued without interruption... The **miraculous cure of diseases of the worst kind could no longer occasion any surprise...** *In the days of Irenaeus, about the end of the 2nd century,* **the resurrection of the dead was very far from being an uncommon event.**

Early church
said 6000 years

"The ancient Christians were animated by a contempt for their present existence and by a just confidence of immortality... The ancient and popular doctrine of the millennium was intimately connected with the second coming of Christ. **As the works of the creation had been finished in six days, the duration in their present state... was fixed to six thousand years.** It was inferred that this long period of labor and contention... would be succeeded by a joyful Sabbath of a thousand years; and that Christ with the triumphant band of saints and the elect who had escaped death... would reign upon earth till the time appointed for the last and general resurrection. So pleasing was this hope to the mind of the believers, that the New Jerusalem, the seat of this blissful kingdom, **was quickly adorned with all the gayest colors of the imagination...**

"From the creation of the world to the birth of Christ (according to) the authority of the Vulgate and of the Hebrew text, it has been determined the... Protestants as well as Catholics prefer a period of about 4000 years... "

Ussher places the time Adam and Eve were driven from the Garden of Eden at about 4004 B.C. This would restrict mankind on earth to about 6000 years. (Of course the calendars are off a few years).

Fossils, etc.

What of the relics and remains which learned men estimate are millions of years old?

◆ Adam and Eve were to *replenish the earth,* Gen. 1:28. Some type of creature had first *"plenished"* it. In the same manner, Noah was commanded to *"re-plenish"* the earth after the flood. It had been *"plenished"* before the flood, Gen. 9: 1.

◆ Not until *God made the sun and moon and divided the day from the night and "let them be for signs, seasons, **and for days and years**,"* (Genesis 1:14), could anyone measure time. No one can count days and years when there was no division of day/night. This was day 4 of Creation Week, before which, time was like an eternal day. *Time* as we know it is but a cog in the wheel of eternity.

I've been there

I studied Chemistry in undergraduate college, and did some practice teaching in the subject. We learned some scientists had treated fossils with the isotope of Carbon 13 and calculated the fossil to be, say, 10 million years old. Another group would treat the same fossil subsequently and determine it was only 1 million years old. That's quite a discrepancy when history can't record any reliable existence of man extending back more than a few thousand years. Hmm.

It appears this terminal generation begun in 1948 will conclude 6000 years of mankind upon the earth. I am of the opinion that the 7th thousand-year-period will be the Millennium Reign of Christ.

So, in a sense, *I have heard a great voice, as of a trumpet saying "write."* That's what my pen has been doing. Hopefully, it is bringing enlightenment to the hearts of many. Perhaps angels may tune their harps while I sit at my desk. Maybe they will even look upon my pen as writing music for them to sing.

Not if but when

If crime was a motivating factor in entering into a cashless society in the early 1980s, terrorism of the 21st century will expedite the process. Jesus Christ warned that certain events would signal his return and end this age. A few have been mentioned: *Nations would be in distress, perplexity and anguish, the earth would be corrupt and filled with violence,* (Luke 21:25, 17:26 and Gen. 6:11).

Additionally, he forewarned of indiscriminate murders: **"Indeed, the time is coming when those who kill you will think they are doing God a service," John 16:2. TLB. Another version: "The time is coming when anyone who kills you will suppose that he is performing a religious duty," NEB.**

To thwart these unselective killings, destruction of property and bio-chemical threats, the world planners will opt for cutting off the terrorists' money supply. The futility of this plan will soon be recognized.

Global conferences will be convened and drastic measures will be formalized. Probably much like Mr. Lederman theorized in his article of 1981: *Confiscate all currency and issue a Universal Card.* The Card will be used for everything—buying, selling, health care, driver's license, passport, etc.

The strategy will be deemed a solution *for only a brief time.* Terrorists who now acquire multiple aliases, driver's licenses and passports, will successfully breach the system. Cards of elderly, retarded and dead folk will be stolen. I.D. theft is already happening. These will be reproduced and sold for whatever the market will bear. The Cards will enable terrorists to pay for flights, food, hotels, flight lessons, etc.

In great perplexity—*"with no passage way out,"* terrorism rampant, violence filling the earth, pestilences (*contagious or infectious epidemics, virulent, devastating diseases that can be destructive or **pernicious**), in divers (many) places*, it seems probable that the world Government will call an Emergency Council. One among them, a gifted communicator, will suggest a last resort for rearranging human landscape. It will necessitate a merging of commerce and religion. Such measures will carry a guarantee to bring "peace and safety" to the earth again. Money will be exchanged for "marks." And, establishment of a One-World religion will require worship of this great communicator, and his spiritual assistant, which they assert will terminate hostilities existing between earth's diverse religions.

The world's ten regions (Dan. 7:20) will give consent to this proposal, and empower him, *the Beast," the false messiah, antichrist, Mr. 666*, to implement it. The edict, which abolishes the use of money, institutes a system of "marks," and requires the worship of a man as God, is recorded in Rev. 13:16-18. (Wicked dictators are referred to as *"beasts, animals,"* etc. in the Bible). A few versions follow:

Revelation 13:16-18

Moreover, it caused everyone, great and small; rich and poor, slave and free, to be branded with a mark on his right hand or forehead, and no one was allowed to buy or sell unless he bore this beast's mark, either name or number. (Here is the key; and anyone who has intelligence may work out the number of the beast. The number represents a man's name, and the numerical value of its letters is six hundred and sixty-six.) NEB.

He also forced everyone, small and great, rich and poor, free and slave, to receive a mark on his right hand or on his forehead, so that no one could buy or sell unless he had the mark, which is the name of the beast or the number of his name. This calls for wisdom. If anyone has insight, let him calculate the number of the beast for it is man's number. His number is 666. NIV.

Then it compels all, small and great, rich and poor, free men and slaves, to receive a mark on their right hands or on their foreheads. The purpose of this is that no one should be able to buy or sell unless he bears the mark of the name of the animal or the number of its name. Understanding is needed here: let every thinking man calculate the number of the animal. It is the number of a man, and its number is six hundred and sixty-six. Phillips Modern English.

He compelled everyone—small and great, rich and poor, slave and citizen—to be branded on the right hand or on the forehead, and made it illegal for anyone to buy or sell anything unless he had been branded with the name of the beast or with the number of its name.

There is need for shrewdness here: if anyone is clever enough he may interpret the number of the beast: it is the number of a man, the number is 666. **Jerusalem Bible.**

He required everyone—great, and small, rich and poor, slave and free— to be tattooed with a certain mark on the right hand or on the forehead. And no one could get a job or even buy in any store without the permit of that mark, which was either the name of the Creature or the code number of his name. Here is a puzzle that calls for careful thought to solve it. Let those who are able, interpret this code: the numerical values of the letters in his name add to 666! **TLB.**

Chapter VIII

Suggestions for Perilous Times

Wisdom dictates that whenever possible, move out of cities. Have an independent supply of water, propane, diesel, kerosene for lamps, old fashioned fire places, extra food (including dry and canned), medicines and if you have no well, store water in bottles.

Many who hold the opinion that the Great Tribulation is very near see a need for owning pre-1965 silver coins, (junk silver), and gold coins, preferably in small denominations, not for investment, but for insurance. If currency is recalled, barter and buying with coins may be a great advantage, as Christians can't take the *"mark of the beast."* A wonderful Christian businessman and friend is one reliable source for silver, gold and *the honest truth as he sees it.* His name and address: Gerald Breyer, 519 22nd Ave. S., Grand Forks, ND 52801, Ph. (888) 417-6324 or (701) 772-0191.

Don't take the "mark"

"And the third angel followed them, saying with a loud voice, If any man worship the beast and his image, and receive his mark in his forehead, or in his hand; The same shall drink of the wine of the wrath of God, which is poured out without mixture into the cup of his indignation; and he shall be tormented with fire and brimstone in the presence of the holy angels, and in the presence of the Lamb: And the smoke of their torment ascendeth up for ever and ever: and they have no rest day nor night, who worship the beast and his image, and whosoever receiveth the mark of his name." Revelation 14:9-11 KJV

Safety is of the Lord. The first 18 Psalms have many great prayers of David against his "terrorist" neighbors. He prays that God will let the evil men fall into the pit they've digged for good men; that they will be caught in the snares they planned for innocent ones, and that the devices they desire to trap people in will work to their own destruction.

"Sensible people will see trouble coming and avoid it, but an unthinking person will walk right into it and regret it later." Prov. 22:3

"Have no anxiety about anything, but in everything by prayer and supplication with thanksgiving let your requests be made known to God. And the peace of God, which passes all understanding will keep your hearts and minds in Christ Jesus," Phil. 4:4-6. RSV.

And finally

The Parish Priest in austerity,
climbed up in the high church steeple,

To be nearer to God, that he might
hand, His word down to the people.

And in sermon script he daily wrote,
what he thought was sent from heaven;

And he dropped it down on the people's
heads, two times one day in seven.

In old age God said, "Come down and
die." And he cried out from the steeple:

"Where art thou, Lord?" and the Lord
replied: "Down here among the
people."

How important to remember that regardless of the perilous times confronting us, He'll never leave us or forsake us. Until that great "catching away," He'll be right down here among His people.

So, let us look forward to greeting the morning of that day that knows neither cloud nor close. Let us make certain we are booked straight through to heaven and insured against collision and explosion. And meanwhile, may we never be so satisfied with earth that we are content to do without heaven.

 SALVATION?

If you sincerely desire to know God:

Admit the problem (You are a sinner.)—
Romans 3:23

Realize the penalty for sin —
Romans 6:23

Understand God's provision for you —
Romans 5:8 John 3:16

Accept God's promise of forgiveness,
and *Confess* your sins,
I John 1:9

Repent (be sorry enough to turn from
your sins.)
II Corinthians 5:17

Believe and *Receive* Christ as your Savior
Romans 10:9-10   John 1:12

If you have received Jesus Christ in your heart
as a result of reading this book, we would like
to pray for you and send you helpful Christian
materials. Please fill in and mail.

NAME _____

ADDRESS _____

CITY _____

STATE _____ ZIP _____

QUOTES

Governor

FOB JAMES, JR.
GOVERNOR

STATE OF ALABAMA
GOVERNOR'S OFFICE
MONTGOMERY

March 11, 1996

"I am happy for the opportunity to speak on Dr. Relfe's behalf, and to recommend her and her work…" I particularly recognize her fine integrity, her outstanding character, and her dedication to humanitarian causes… which are used to uplift society both here and abroad in the name of our Lord… **Dr. Relfe is a friend from whom I have sought guidance during times that I've had to make hard decisions…"**

Fob James, Jr.

Auditor

I can truthfully testify that Dr. Relfe is a lady of extremely high ethical standards. In all of my experience as an auditor I have never seen operational efficiencies such as exist at League of Prayer. Administrative costs are the lowest of any nonprofit organization's expenses I have ever seen. The financial records are impeccable…"

Steve Richardson, CPA
Tuscaloosa, Alabama

"I believe this League of Prayer is born of the Holy Spirit and no man can stop it...
I believe God will use you and this League of Prayer to change America and the whole world."

David Yonggi Cho, Pastor
Yoido Full Gospel Church
 Seoul, Korea

October 26, 1985

...Dr. Mary Stewart Relfe is a person of unquestioned integrity, ability-diligence in the work of the Lord...
In the opinion of many civic and religious leaders, Dr. Relfe is one of the most remarkable ladies of our time. She is highly educated, and most sensitive to the leading of the Holy Spirit...

Willard Cantelon
9424 Lost Trail Way
Potomac, MD 20854

■ BOOKS AND TAPES ■
by
Mary Stewart Relfe

☐	Prophetic Fallout of 9-11	$8.95
☐	Ghosts at the Wesley House	$7.95
☐	The New Money System	$8.95
☐	Cure of All Ills—Revival	$9.95
☐	Should You Take a Little Wine?	$4.00
☐	Make Known His Deeds	$3.00
☐	My Sojourn in Heaven	$7.95
☐	League of Prayer Newsletter	FREE

UNFORGETTABLE VIDEOS
Order on next page

Dr. David Yonggi Cho and Dr. Mary Stewart Relfe
on
Dr. Cho's visit in heaven
Dr. Cho's assistant—3 days in heaven
Prayer life at Yoido Full Gospel Church
Excerpts of Prayer Convention

■■ UNFORGETTABLE VIDEOS ■■

☐ **Interview wtih Dr. Cho** $20.00
Dr. Relfe interviews Dr. Cho who shares his
astounding vision of heaven, his prayer life,
etc. 35 min.

☐ **Let Us Pray** $20.00
Prayer and Praise by Dr. Relfe at *America's
Call to Prayer Convention*. Endorsements of
League of Prayer and Dr. Relfe by Dr. Cho and
Dr. Vaudie Lambert. 34 min.

☐ **Prayer & Miracles** $35.00
Excerpts of *America's Call to Prayer
Convention*. Dr. Relfe prays and Dr. Cho
shares some incredible highlights of his
ministry. 75 minutes

■■■ AUDIO TAPES ■■■

by Mary Stewart Relfe

☐ **I Saw Children in Hell** $5.00
☐ **Ravens Cry — People Pray** $5.00
☐ Please send Book/Tape List
☐ Postage/Handling $3.00

TOTAL ORDER ___$_____

Name

Address

City/State/Zip

☐ Check ☐ Money Order

Charge My Credit Card ☐ Visa ☐ MasterCard

Card Number: _____

Expiration Date: _____

Signature on Card: _____

LEAGUE OF PRAYER

P.O. Box 680310
Prattville, AL 36068

Phone 334 361 8497
FAX 334 361 9588

E-mail: *LofPinc@aol.com*
www.LeagueofPrayer.org